UI

IN

PRAYER

by

Martin Reardon

SPCK/CTS

First published 1979

SPCK
Holy Trinity Church
Marylebone Road
London NW1 4DU

and

The Catholic Truth Society
38/40 Eccleston Square
London SW1V 1PD

ISBN 0 281 03749 3(SPCK)
0 85183 298 9(CTS)

UNITY
IN
PRAYER

'What no eye has seen, nor ear heard,
nor the heart of man conceived
what God has prepared for those who love him,
God has revealed to us through the Spirit.'

1 Corinthians 2, 9

PRAYER

True Prayer begins essentially in our response to God. We catch a glimpse, a scent, a touch, a taste, a call, and we respond. It does not begin as a lonely human search, a battering at a door which will not open. St Augustine wrote: 'You would not seek me if you had not already found me.' It is true that later on, often for long periods at a time, God seems to have disappeared and we struggle on apparently without him. But initially and essentially this is not so. Jesus did not first order his disciples to pray. His disciples first expressed the wish to respond to God in this way, and they asked Jesus to teach them how to pray. Prayer becomes a duty only after we have received it as a gift. It is our duty to respond and to persevere in responding to the gift of prayer.

We can put this another way by saying that we can only pray through the power of the Holy Spirit. It is the Spirit who teaches us to respond to God in prayer, who enables us to become new creatures in Christ, and so to share in his work of creation and redemption.

In prayer God takes the initiative. In prayer therefore our attitude must primarily be one of waiting upon him. Alas, prayer is not always seen as this. Too many people attempt not only to take the initiative in prayer, but fail to get beyond a self-centred, or at least a man-centred, concept of asking God for things. If they at first receive what they ask for, they may experience a dangerously self-centred elation that God is on their side. Such an experience will need to be deepened and broadened if it is not to lead to eventual disillusionment. If they fail to get what they asked for, some Christians give up prayer. Those who continue to pray in this situation often find that prayer itself becomes an extra burden and yet another weary duty in a life of burdens and duties. This is not prayer as it has to be, but very few are the Christians who have not experienced such a period of dry dissatisfaction in their life or such temptations to give it all up.

Yet other Christians treat prayer as a tranquillizer or temporary escape from the hard realities of life. One Christian said that she regarded God as her own personal armchair. When life was hard she sank back into him for comfort, rest and reassurance. This view too is clearly inadequate. It is self-centred. It separates prayer from life. We should not turn to prayer simply for a little help in the real and major task of living. William Temple wrote: 'People are always thinking that conduct is supremely important, and that because prayer helps it, therefore prayer is good. That is true so far as it goes, still truer is it to say that worship is of supreme importance and conduct tests it. Conduct tests how much of yourself was in the worship you gave to God' (*Christian Faith and Life* by William Temple, SCM Press, p. 19).

Prayer is the consciousness of living with God, especially the struggle to harmonize our wills with his. It therefore relates to whatever we devote our energy and life to, to all our inmost desires and wishes. It has at least two risks. Either we express only what *we* want and become disappointed when we do not get it. Or we piously mouth the classic prayers of the Church, we make 'Thy will be done' into a platitude; and then jump into bed and think about what we really want. If we fall into the first trap, there is every danger that we will give up all practice of prayer. If we fall into the second, whether we realize it or not, we are hypocrites. In neither case is there any harmonization of wills. In the former case God's will is ignored. In the latter case it is insulated from daily life and our wills. Real prayer is the exhilarating struggle between these two wills. Such prayer touches every aspect of human life. It becomes the centre and pivot of our lives, and can never again become peripheral, an activity we relegate to a few set times and places. Set times and places of prayer are very important and provide an anchor in a sea of total prayerlessness. Yet as prayer develops all our work, all our life is directed by and to God, and so our very work and life is an expression of our prayer – in a profound sense *is* our prayer.

Liturgy

What has been written about private prayer also applies to corporate worship. Corporate worship is the shared prayer of a Christian community. It should both focus the common concerns of the individuals who participate in it, and also build up a sense of community by the sharing of those concerns in and with Christ. It is very easy for corporate worship to become so formalized that the participants find it difficult to relate it to the concerns and preoccupations of their everyday life. Those who come to public worship merely to escape from the daily struggle will accentuate the division between life and worship by approving it.

This is not to say that private prayer and corporate worship must have as their only themes the earthly desires and concerns of men. Christianity, and therefore the prayer and worship of Christians, is to do with the Kingdom of God. Our concerns are to be transformed and transcended in the concern and will of God. Yet Jesus taught that the Kingdom of God is already appearing among us, though it can never be contained in the concerns of this world. He taught, so St Matthew's Gospel tells us, that we should be judged on what we had done, for example, in feeding the hungry, visiting the sick and clothing the naked, for our active concern and care for the poor is to be a mirror of our concern and care for him. Our life of activity is but a reflection of our life of prayer. Our whole life is the expression of our conviction that the risen Christ is present with us in the Spirit and that all we do is done by his grace within us, and is done in union with all Christians who together seek direction from him and in their turn direct all that they are and do and say towards God.

There is one single language of praying and living. The Christian who truly cares for his neighbour will bring the joys, sorrows and needs of his neighbour into private and corporate prayer. The Christian who truly prays for and with his neighbour will want to share his joys and sorrows, and will do what he can to meet his needs. The Christian who truly cares for his neighbour and truly prays will have a style of life through which other people see God at work transforming the world. Prayer and worship give a proper context and orientation for activity. Without prayer and worship Christian activism is liable to degenerate into a humanitarianism without direction. Without action Christian prayer and worship is liable to degenerate into other – wordly escapism. If we allow our praying and our acting to flow into each other, then the Holy Spirit can make our life into a harmonious stream that both reflects God and also brings life to others. To pray is to live and to live is to pray.

UNITY

'For he has made known to us . . . his purpose which he set forth in Christ as a plan for the fulness of time, to unite all things in him, things in heaven and things on earth.'

Ephesians 1, 10

We usually date the beginning of the modern movement towards Christian Unity from 1910 when a missionary conference was held in Edinburgh. The search for Christian unity clearly had as its motive the desire for more effective mission. Missionaries had gone out from Europe and North America to preach the Gospel of the reconciliation of all men in Christ, and they had preached it in competition with one another. Their very actions and competitive existence as separate denominations contradicted their Gospel of reconciliation. 'By this all men will know that you are my disciples, if you have love for one another.' (Jn 13, 35.) Historically the immediate and ostensible cause of the modern ecumenical movement was a missionary motive – 'That they may all be one .. that the world may believe . . .' (Jn 17, 21).

A secondary reason for the coming together of the Churches is often given, especially in new housing areas. It is that scarce Christian resources can be used more effectively if the different denominations will come together to share what they have. In this regard the Sharing of Church Buildings Act, passed by Parliament in 1969, marked a significant step forward. It enables Christians of different traditions legally to use one another's buildings for worship in certain situations where this had not previously been possible, and from this many further steps in co-operation have been made.

Behind the missionary motive for Christian unity is an even more profound reason; that God himself is Unity in Trinity. The Abbé Paul Couturier, a French Roman Catholic priest who died in 1954, constantly reminded Christians of this in the last twenty years of his life. He loved to quote our Lord's prayer for unity as recorded in Jn 17, 21: 'that they may all be one: even as thou, Father, art in me, and I in thee, that they also may be in us, so that the world may believe that thou hast sent me'. The sort of relationship which helps people to see Christ, and in which all Christians are called to share, is the relationship which exists between the Father and Jesus Christ. The only way to find this kind of unity, as Paul Couturier constantly reminded us, is to pray for it in union with Christ's own prayer to the Father (Jn 17).

The unity for which Paul Couturier taught us to pray was primarily seen as the unity of all Christians. The Week of Prayer for Christian Unity, which he did not found, but which has been so closely linked with his name, was for many years seen primarily as a week of prayer for the reunion of Christendom. Yet, as we have seen, from the Edinburgh Conference of 1910 onwards this Christian unity has been seen by many not simply as an end in itself, but also as a means of bringing all mankind into unity with God through Christ and his Church. Paul Couturier himself understood it in this wider context. Others also saw that Christian unity could not be dissociated from a wider human unity. The mining towns in the Copperbelt drew together Africans from different tribes and cultures, speaking different languages. The workers had a desperate human need for a sense of community. The Christian missionaries could have helped to bring it to them. Instead the different denominations set up rival church communities and so brought further division. We have only to mention Northern Ireland to remember the tragic link there between Christian divisions and civil strife. Christian unity cannot in the end be dissociated from the unity of mankind. In the 1960s people began to talk of 'secular ecumenism'. This was concerned primarily with the divisions which existed within the human race rather than with the divisions within the Christian Churches. They were talking about the war in Biafra, with exploitation in Latin America, the structures of world trade which kept the West wealthy and the so-called 'third world' poor, the confrontation between black and white in Africa and in our own country, and about the rights of women. These and many similar issues were seen to be the concern of Christians. These concerns for human unity were therefore included in material for prayer during the Week of Prayer for Christian Unity alongside prayer for unity among Christians. Indeed so successful is the Week of Prayer for Christian Unity that other organizations have initiated other weeks of prayer at other times of the year, as, for example, the Week of Prayer for World Peace.

What is the justification for including concern for the unity of mankind in a week devoted to prayer for Christian unity? In Christ all merely human barriers are broken down. 'There is neither Jew nor Greek, there is neither slave nor free, there is neither male nor female; for you are all one in Christ Jesus' (Gal 3, 28, cf Col 3, 11). From the foundation of the world God's plan was 'to unite all things in Christ, things in heaven and things on earth' (Eph 1, 10, cf Col 1, 20). The Church has an important place in this vision of ultimate cosmic unity as we can see in the letters to the Ephesians and Colossians. The Church's task was to make God's plan known to the whole cosmos (Eph 3, 10). A similar vision inspired Paul's earlier letters 'God was in Christ reconciling the world to himself . . . and entrusting to us the message of reconciliation' (2 Cor 5, 19). The Church, the whole people of God, shares in the ministry of Jesus Christ which is to bring all mankind into unity with the Father.

What sort of unity?

This unity and reconciliation is not a unity and reconciliation to be worked out on the basis of compromise. It was not any sort of peace at any price that Jesus came to bring. Indeed at one point the Gospel records that he claimed to bring division rather than peace (Mt 10, 34). The peace, unity and reconciliation brought by Christ is precisely unity with the Father, and this inevitably involves conflict and confrontation with all that is evil in ourselves, in the Church and in the world. Clearly the Church needs to pray for true reconciliation and unity within itself, if it is to be an effective agent of Christ's reconciliation in the world at large. Clearly also the Church needs to pray for justice, peace and reconciliation in the secular world and for the tearing down of all barriers which separate man from God and therefore man from man.

How does the reunion of the Christian Church properly relate to the reconciliation of all mankind to God? The simple explanation, that *first* the Churches must be re-united and then the one Church will be a more effective reconciling instrument in a divided world, is not satisfactory to everyone for two reasons. First there are people who fear that the reunion which some Christians are working for will be an unsatisfactory compromise enforced on all Christians as a kind of uniformity. Such a superficial uniformity, they claim, will be no basis from which to work for the unity of mankind. On the contrary the wonderful variety of culture and gifts must all be retained in the harmony of God's Kingdom. We must take note of this fear. Each Christian almost inevitably imagines a united Christian Church in the form of his own Church. Consciously or unconsciously we all work and pray to that end. We need constantly to remind ourselves that the unity we seek is God's and therefore inevitably transcends our personal imagining. The Abbé Paul Couturier himself evolved a formula of prayer which avoids a merely human uniformity. He taught us to pray for the unity which Christ wills to come in the way he wills it to come.

The second reason is that many people fear that Christians are so concerned to dot every 'i' and cross every 't' before union, that it will never be achieved. They see that time spent on searching for unity among Christians has been time lost in spreading the Gospel or working for God's kingdom of justice and peace in the world at large. Mission and evangelism or justice and peace is the primary object. Christian unity is merely a means to that end. Mission comes first. Unity, if it comes at all, will come as a result of co-operation in mission. We must agree with this view that mission and evangelization is a primary task of the Christian community; and that the search for reunion must not hinder this. However we cannot accept the despair of any closer Christian unity this side of the grave.

The Gospel demands that we share in Christ's work of reconciliation in bringing true peace and justice to his world. Christian integrity demands that his same reconciling love be embodied in a reconciled Church. The missionaries at Edinburgh in 1910 discovered that Christian unity was required in order that Christian mission might be more effective. We are discovering that Christians have become so closely tied to differing church structures, ways of worship and expressions of doctrine that a profound renewal of the Church's life and mission is needed in order to bring us to unity.

Co-operation in mission now may help to bring the separated Churches to a proper sense of priorities, deeper renewal and growing unity.

This is not to say that unity among the Churches is not urgently needed. Some Christians have prayed that it may come in 'God's good time'. God's good time is now. God wills Christian unity now. It is the sin of Christians who cannot respond in complete openness to God and to each other which hinders unity. Constant prayer along can overcome our sin so that God may renew the life of his Church at once both in mission and in unity.

UNITY IN PRAYER

May they all be one: even as thou, Father, art in me, and I in thee, that they may be in us, that the world may believe that thou hast sent me.

John 17, 21

We may summarize the relationship between prayer and unity as follows:

1. God is the source and goal of the true unity of the Church, of mankind and of the universe.
2. Prayer begins when we respond to God's prior love for us. In this response a two-sided relationship begins between God and ourselves. In this relationship our wills are graduallv harmonized with his.
3. Worship is corporate prayer, the corporate expression of the growing relationship of all those who are trying to respond to God, and therefore to each other, in prayer.
4. Therefore worship and prayer are channels by which God's reconciling love flows (a) into me, and heals my own internal contradictions and insecurities; (b) into my relationships with other Christians and strengthens and blesses them; and (c) into all human relationships and creates one single new humanity in Christ (Eph 2, 15).
5. This prayer and worship cannot be dissociated from life and action. For the Christian prayer and worship find expression in life and action. Life and action that are founded in prayer themselves become living and acted prayer.

There will be times when we focus more consciously on our relationship with God in prayer and worship. Without such special times of prayer and worship there is a danger that the rest of what we do in our life may lose its direction. The Week of Prayer for Christian Unity from 18th–25th January is such a time. Each year almost half a million copies of a prayer leaflet are sold in Britain. For over a century evangelical Christians have devoted the first full week of January to praying for the evangelization of the world. Some Christians pray for Christian unity particularly at Pentecost.

Prayer for unity should continue to include concerted and persistent intercession for Christian unity, for all those individuals, groups, and organizations working for reunion, and for current schemes and plans. In the spirit of Paul Couturier it should be prayer that God's unity may come in the way he wishes it to come. Such prayer is already offered regularly at set times in various Cathedrals and other centres. Perhaps new centres might also gather people to pray regularly for the unity of the Church. A particularly appropriate time for such prayer is Thursday evening in union with Christ's 'high priestly prayer' for unity recorded in John 17.

Such regular prayer might also include informed intercession for all Churches in all lands. The Fifth Assembly of the World Council of Churches meeting in Nairobi in 1975 recommended 'that all Churches should encourage and assist their members in regular and informed intercession for the other churches.' In response to this request an Ecumenical Prayer Cycle has been published with Roman Catholic participation entitled *For All God's People* (SPCK and CTS). We hope it will be widely used in private and group prayer and in corporate worship.

Prayer for unity should not stop at prayer for Christians. We should see intercession for man in all his physical, social, political and economic as well as in his spiritual need as part of our prayer for the reconciliation of the whole universe to God. The Revd John Smith gives an account of how one local Council of Churches in Sheffield meets regularly to pray for the needs of society in its locality.

'Has a local council of churches any point? The frustration of meeting to plan yet another united service had become acute. I was all for packing in this ecumenical game which always ended in a goal-less draw. But two things prompted us to think again. First was a call to nationwide evangelism, and secondly an inner conviction that when the church does not know what to do, it should pray.

'Those two statements sound contradictory, but the truth is that we as churches in the lower Sharrow area had little right to evangelize in our neighbourhood. The congregations are often eclectic, or worse still, living locally but withdrawn from the "feel" of things. How do you reverse this trend? How turn the church inside, outside? The way we are committed to in the next year or so is prayer together about once a quarter. At these meetings, we ask someone to hold up a mirror into society – our local society, and so far we have looked at provisions for old people, work amongst youngsters, the vandal, probation work. Then we have prayer. The effect? The mirror gave sight to the blind! And so our prayer always has about it a note of deep repentance because we know so little about the people next door to all our churches, repentance because, although we say we care, so few people are prepared to give an evening away from the television and the "nicer" meetings. Our prayer has also led to heightened expectancy – what God has to do if our neighbourhoods are to be renewed.

'We feel we are being stripped for action – action where evangelism and social concern go out together, hand in hand.'

Praise and thanksgiving

In the section on Prayer it was observed that asking is only one part of prayer. The charismatic movement is reminding us of the centrality of praise and adoration in worship and prayer. This helps to redress the tendency of our prayer to focus too much on ourselves and on man's concerns and divisions. Instead it emphasizes the priority and unity of God in everything. There is an increasing demand for Christians to come together, sometimes in quite large numbers, simply to celebrate and to praise God. Such events have brought thousands of Christians together in Manchester's Free Trade Hall and London's Trafalgar Square. This occasional coming together in praise is particularly attractive for young people when it includes popular music, dance and drama; but there is much to be said for involving all age groups in this. Such events can sometimes be linked to a pilgrimage to a place of popular devotion.

Thought could also be given to arranging such gatherings of praise at major festivals. It has been customary in Britain for Christians of different traditions to worship together in the Week of Prayer for Christian Unity and on Good Friday, and we hope that such customs will grow. Could we not also meet to celebrate at some time during the major festivals of Christmas, Epiphany, Easter, Ascension and Pentecost?

Near to praise is thanksgiving. Any meeting for praise on the major festivals would be bound to include united thanksgiving to God for what he has done for us all in Jesus Christ. Yet how often when we meet together as Christians from different traditions do we corporately thank God and each other for the riches God has given to each of our particular Churches. This is a delicate area – we may not agree on what we value most highly in our own and in other traditions; but the attempt to discover this could lead to a great enrichment of inter-church understanding, trust and appreciation. We can also thank God for the measure of unity we have already been given.

Such expression of praise and gratitude need not, of course, be confined to the traditions of the Churches. We can also meet to praise and thank God for the diversity of cultures, peoples and races, and for the harmony that already exists between them. In Slough Christians have come together on May Bank Holiday to celebrate the World of Work.

One event which gave an occasion for a national expression of united gratitude was the unveiling in October 1977 in Westminster Abbey at the tomb of Queen Elizabeth I and Queen Mary of a memorial to all martyrs of conscience. When Lady Fisher unveiled the memorial, gratitude was expressed for the witness of both Catholic and Protestant martyrs at the time of the Reformation.* The occasion also obviously provided an opportunity for mutual admission of wrongs done to others.

Admission of sin is clearly an authentic part of prayer and should have its rightful place in united prayer and worship. It brings however particular difficulties and dangers. Most groups, even groups where great mutual trust has been built up, will think it right to avoid individual confession in group prayer; though some groups may dare to find a place for it. Yet even if individual confession is confined to formal expression, how specific can corporate confession be? To what extent is it appropriate for me to confess the sins of earlier generations, or even the sins of my own group or church, if I myself honestly believe that I am not personally guilty of them? It is as well to be aware of these problems, and of the differing attitudes Christians take to them, when we plan any corporate act of worship involving confession.

At the heart of the Roman Catholic mass is a prayer for Christian unity. Indeed the regular worship of our separate churches often contains prayers both for the unity of the church and for the unity of all mankind. In sharing in these prayers we are

*The address, given on this occasion by the Dean of Westminster, is published in *One in Christ*, 1978, No. 1.

joining in spirit with Christians of other churches praying similar prayers in their traditional worship. If our prayer for unity is to attain depth we need to enter into the ways of worship of other churches. To enter each other's traditions of worship helps us to meet each other at a spiritual level. It is not always easy to enter these traditions at first; but it can be rewarding. Olive Wyon tells the story of an Anglo-Catholic layman who said in a small group: 'I used to be very "spiky!" but one day I heard a Nonconformist pray, and all my spikes fell off!' (*Praying for Unity*, Olive Wyon, p. 24). It is sometimes more appropriate for all the churches in a neighbourhood to join in the traditional worship of one of their number, instead of creating a form of worship familiar to none of them. This becomes very clear in the case of the celebration of the sacraments of baptism and the eucharist. These are at the heart of most of our traditions. In some traditions we are not all permitted always to receive communion, though this is becoming increasingly possible. Even so non-communicating attendance can be turned into a painful prayer for unity. In such circumstances when intercommunion is not possible, some may prefer to meet in a less formal 'fellowship meal'.

In a number of different places clergy and ministers meet regularly for prayer. This has happened for a number of years in Gainsborough in Lincolnshire. There each morning in a town centre church united prayers have been based on the *Daily Office* produced by the Joint Liturgical Group. Extempore prayer is also made. Such regular prayer leads to understanding, and this has its effect both on church congregations and also on the wider community.

The daily offices in the Christian Church began in the first centuries as meditations upon Scripture. Hundreds of primarily lay ecumenical groups have begun in recent years for Bible study and prayer. Through returning to source in this way many Christians have found refreshment and renewal together in unity and mission.

We have earlier emphasized the link between prayer and life. Some of these informal prayer groups have begun when Christians of different traditions in a neighbourhood or street have met together, perhaps through a local Council of Churches. They may have decided not only to pray together, but also to share their talents and even some of their possessions not only with each other, but also with others in the neighbourhood who might need them. Some such groups have remained informal and ceased to exist as people have moved away. Others have formed themselves into more permanent ecumenical communities.

CONCLUSION

If what has been written about prayer and unity is right, we should expect prayer to be at the heart of the whole movement for Christian unity for two reasons. First of all it is one activity that *all* Christians can share. Not all of us are academic theologians who can help to produce agreed statements of doctrine. Not all of us are administrators who can work out schemes of reunion. Not all of us are leaders who can discuss and ratify or reject such schemes. But we can all pray.

Secondly prayer is central to the whole ecumenical movement because it is, or should be, an activity which recognizes the priority of God without any possibility of misunderstanding. 'The way to the union of Christendom does not lie through committee rooms (though there is a task of formulation to be done there). It lies through personal union with the Lord so deep and real as to be comparable with his union with the Father'. *(Readings in St John's Gospel*, William Temple, p. 237.)

It has been said that the mature Christian needs three conversions in his life: (1) Conversion to God in Christ; (2) Conversion to the Church; and (3) Conversion to the World. True prayer begins in conversion to God in Christ. It grows into worship and we discover unity in prayer when we are converted to the Church, to all the others who have been converted to God in Christ, whether we agree with them entirely or not, whether we find them attractive or not. It expands into every aspect of our living and acting when we are converted to the world for which Jesus Christ lived and died and rose again; and when all our living and acting become the expression of our prayer and worship. In this threefold way is discovered the integrity of true unity in prayer. As Christians of all traditions enter more deeply into this kind of unity in prayer, so the unity of Christ's Church will become more clearly visible, and the Church become a more effective instrument of God's reconciling love for the world.

Printed in England by Staples Printers St Albans Limited
at The Priory Press